Sample Mutual Fund Portfolios

Written and edited by Joseph Sheeley, Ph.D.

Copyright 2022. All rights reserved.

Sample Mutual Fund Portfolios

Copyright © 2022 by Joseph Sheeley
All rights reserved.

ISBN: 9798332238499

No portion of this work may be reproduced, stored in a retrieval system, or transmitted in any form or by any means, including electronic, mechanical, photocopy, recording, or otherwise, without the express written permission of the author. For information regarding permission for use, contact the author via smallivy.wordpress.com.

This edition first printing.

Introduction

If you're like a lot of people, you're probably finding yourself in a position where you need to choose investments and develop a portfolio in your 401k plan when your family has never done any investing. Human resources at your new job just gave you a form and told you to hand in back in a couple of days. Or maybe you've heard how important investing is to building a strong financial future and you want to start putting away some money from your work, but you just don't know where to start. Maybe you've started a 529 plan for your kids or even an educational IRA and now need to figure out how to invest the money you're contributing.

How you invest and in what you invest depends on your goals, your time period for investing, and your risk tolerance. In virtually all cases you'll use mutual funds, but there are thousands of different mutual funds out there. How do you get the knowledge of which funds to choose, how much money to invest in each, and how to manage your portfolio as you get closer to your goal when you'll use the money?

The purpose of this mini book is to give some of the basics of developing a mutual fund portfolio. To do this, example portfolios are provided for different scenarios. Rather than just give a list of funds, however, and say "Do this," the reasons behind why each portfolio is built in a certain way are given. How the portfolio is maintained and adjusted as your situation changes is also discussed. The reader is not expected to just choose a portfolio from the examples and duplicate it.

The goal is to teach you how to construct and maintain a portfolio so that you can then tweak the examples to meet your special needs.

Mutual fund investing is really very easy and requires very little time. The steps are to first develop a library of mutual funds (your 401k plan administrator does this for you), determine your allocations – what percentage of your portfolio you want to put into each mutual funds – then fund your portfolio accordingly. The main knowledge needed is how to develop a library of mutual funds and then how to determine allocations based on your risk tolerance and goals. This mini book teaches you how to develop your library and then presents sample portfolios for different needs.

The book is purposely not very long and would be easy to read in a hour (or two, if one really studies the materials), but really you could just read the first chapter to get the basics and then find the portfolio example that matches your special need and start there, whether it is investing for retirement, saving up for a big expense, developing an account to provide extra income, or prepare for college expenses. Once you're investing you may then return to look at a different type of account or to improve your understanding of the methodology so you can tune existing accounts to best meet your needs. I've no doubt this may be a book you keep on your phone or tablet, ready to review when you have a spare moment in your day. So, sit back and relax as we start with the basics. Welcome to the world of investing!

Chapter 1: Building a Mutual Fund Library

There are hundreds if not thousands of mutual funds available. Running a mutual fund is a lucrative business, so many people do just that. The more money a manager puts under management, the more he can collect in fees, so every company is trying to lure in customers. This means there is lots of advertising with each fund company claiming they are the best choice. Every fund is special with super-human abilities to pick the right stocks at just the right time.

But the truth is that the investments within all funds in a given segment of the markets will perform about the same over long periods of time if the manager just invests the money and leaves it alone. All US large cap funds will see their portfolios return about 10% annualized. International large cap funds will return about the same. Small cap funds will see returns of 12% to 15%. The difference in returns will be due to 1. bad market timing by managers and 2. fund costs. So, finding funds for your portfolio comes down to selecting the fund from each segment of the markets that is managed well and has low costs.

We are not going to buy any fund where the money manager has free reign to decide where to invest. We don't believe anyone is going to know where to invest at any given time to beat the markets and we don't want to leave our money with people who are going to try. That is a sure recipe for high costs and returns that lag the averages. Instead we are going to purposely allocate our money to funds in different areas of the market and just let each manager invest within his segment. We therefore will only invest in funds that cover specific segments of the markets and then combine those funds in such a way to give us appropriate exposure to each of those market segments.

We use historical data to be our guide on how different areas of the markets will behave. We understand that we will not know what a particular segment of the market will do over the next several years but we expect that if we invest long enough the average returns will be about what they were in the past. Think of this like predicting the weather in different regions. You don't know what the temperatures will be like in any given week or how much rain and snow you'll get, but by looking at the past you can get a good estimate of what the average temperatures will be like for a given month of the year and the range of rainfall totals will be. In particular, you can predict which areas will tend to be warmer and which will tend to be wetter than others. Likewise, using historical data you can predict about how a given segment of the markets will perform on average over long periods of time and how volatile they will be, particularly in comparison with other segments of the market.

We will only invest in certain areas and types of securities, having learned which are suitable for investment and which are not. These are areas where we can expect to see growth and returns beyond inflation We also use history to guide how long we need to be invested in each segment of the market to get a positive return that we can predict, at least within an expected range. If we don't have at least that much time to invest, and we really need to pull the money out at a given point in the future, we won't invest in those areas of the markets.

For example, if we hold large US stocks for a period of 10 to 15 years, we can expect to see a positive return and for that return to be between about 5 and 15%. Looking back at several periods of time over the last 120 years where we have data, during most 10 to 15 years periods large US stocks saw returns within this range. Large US stocks would therefore be a suitable investment if we have 10 to 15 years to invest. If we really needed to pull the money out in two years, however, large US stocks would not be suitable because we could end up with less money that we started with. In that case, a bank CD would be the better investment since we'd have a predictable positive return.

Doing a quick survey, we come up with the following areas that are possible investments:

1. Large US Stocks
2. Small and Medium US Stocks
3. Large Non-US Stocks in Developed Countries
4. Small and Medium Non-US Stocks in Developed Countries
5. Stocks in Developing Countries
6. US Government Bonds (Federal and State)
7. US Corporate Bonds (investment Grade)
8. US Corporate Bonds (Junk)

9. Non-US Bonds (Investment Grade)
10. Non-US Bonds (Junk)
11. US Real Estate
12. Non-US Real Estate, Developed Countries
13. Non-US Real Estate, Developing Countries

Note that there are areas we do not include. We don't include cryptocurrencies. While these are very popular right now, there is no fundamental reason that they will grow in value, so they are not included. We don't include commodities since their return is unpredictable and they will not beat inflation over time. We don't include things like pop art, collectible cars, and other collectibles because they would tend to increase in value only for a time period and then decline. Elvis' comb might receive a high value today, but will probably not in 50 years when everyone who knew of Elvis has died. Note, we might consider a fund that invested in fine arts since those can have staying power for decades or even centuries.

We generally want to make investments is many areas since doing so means we'll always have something that is doing well and will reduce the level of fluctuations in our portfolio. (This is called *diversification*). If we buy a large US stock fund and hold it for 30 years, we'll see returns of about 10% annualized (7% after inflation). We'll see the same if we buy a large non-US stock fund. If we put all of our money in one or the other and waited 30 years, we'd see about the same result at the end regardless of which fund we chose, but the portfolio performance from year-to-year would vary. If we split the money and bought both funds, we'd still end up with about the same returns but the changes in our portfolio value would be less each year since one area might be going up when the other was going down. This would mean that we'd see fewer jarring drops along the way, the kind that might worry us and make us sell everything at just the wrong time. It would also mean that if we did need to use some of the money early for some reason, it would be more likely that we wouldn't be in the middle of a big drop in portfolio value when we needed the money.

Now, we could probably find one or two funds that invest in each of the areas we listed and make up our library from those, but that would be overly complicated. Mutual fund companies have created funds that combine areas for us, so we don't need to go out and buy funds in every area. We really want to have a fairly simple portfolio, so we'll want to combine areas where it makes sense. In some cases, however, we may want separate funds so that we have a little more control of how much is invested in a given area. For example, we might want to concentrate in corporate bonds for their higher yields, so we may want to have separate corporate and government bond funds rather than just buy a general bond fund that invests in both. Other times, there is no reason for separate funds.

Managed or unmanaged (index) funds

In finding specific funds for our library, one choice that we'll have is whether we will choose managed or unmanaged funds for each area. In many cases we'll choose index funds since they have lower fees and eliminate the danger of having a fund manager who needlessly trades and possibly misses a big opportunity because he was trying to time the markets. In some areas, however, it does help to have an expert hand to choose in what to invest and what to avoid. For example, in developing market funds, there are some areas of the world where the risk from social upheaval is just too great, so we don't want to be invested there. In this case having someone who studies markets and decides which ones present the best opportunities and which ones should be avoided makes sense. There may also be areas in which we want to invest where there are no index funds. In these cases, we may end up with a managed fund as the only choice.

Fund companies

For index funds in basic areas of the markets, such as an S&P500 fund or a US small cap fund, there are several choices that are basically all the same and we can choose a fund company for other reasons such as customer service, fees, and convenience. If we are investing using a brokerage account, we can basically buy funds from any company. For some, it may make sense to have an account directly with a fund company because they may then offer perks like commission-free trading in their funds. For others, investing from a brokerage fund may simplify things.

For this book, we will use Vanguard funds to build our library. This doesn't mean we're recommending these funds over those from other fund companies such as Charles Schwab. It is just to provide examples of specific funds that the reader can study further to see how they're composed and how they behave rather than refer to generic funds. When you're choosing which fund company to use (and whether you'll open a full brokerage account or not), review what each company has to offer and make the choice that makes the most sense for you. If we use a Vanguard fund in our sample portfolios but you can get a similar fund from another company more easily or cheaply, by all means make the substitution.

Forming the library

We've reached the point where we're ready to assemble our library. These are the possible investment choices we'll draw from in forming our portfolio. Using primarily Vanguard funds, here is the list we'll use:

1. Large US Stocks

For large US stocks, certainly an index is the way to go. Choices here are the S&P500 fund or just the Large Cap Index fund. We could also use the Value Index and the Growth Index to provide the opportunity to skew towards growth or value. The Windsor Fund is a managed large value fund that has done well and has low fees. There is also the choice of the Total Stock Market Index, which actually buys everything, but since it weights by capitalization, we'll end up with a lot more money invested in the large companies than the small ones with this choice. We'll keep all of these options since there are scenarios where we'll want to use each.

2. Small and Medium US Stocks

In mid-caps we have the Mid-Cap Index. For small caps we choose the Small-Cap Index, although an issue with investing here is that, again because we're capitalization weighted, most of the money we'll put in this index will be invested in stocks that are almost mid-caps. We also include a managed fund, the Vanguard Explorer Fund, which has a value slant to it to give us options.

3. Large Non-US Stocks in Developed Countries
4. Small and Medium Non-US Stocks in Developed Countries
5. Stocks in Developing Countries

For international, we're going to use the Vanguard Core International Stock Fund, which actually includes some emerging markets exposure as well, as way to get broad exposure to different markets. We're also going to add the Vanguard Emerging Markets Select Stock Fund as a way to concentrate on emerging markets.

6. US Government Bonds (Federal and State)
7. US Corporate Bonds (investment Grade)
8. US Corporate Bonds (Junk)
9. Non-US Bonds (Investment Grade)
10. Non-US Bonds (Junk)

We're going to simplify things with bonds by using the Total Bond Market Index and a Total International Bond Index. We'll also add the High Yield Corporate Bond fund to provide the ability to tilt towards junk bonds as needed.

    11. US Real Estate
    12. Non-US Real Estate, Developed Countries
    13. Non-US Real Estate, Developing Countries

We'll use REIT funds to get exposure to real estate. Here we'll use the Vanguard Real Estate Index for US real estate and the Global ex-U.S. Real Estate Index for international real-estate.

Our final library is therefore as follows:

Large US Stocks:
Vanguard S&P500 Index
Vanguard Large Cap Index
Vanguard Growth Index
Vanguard Value Index
Vanguard Total Stock Market Index
Vanguard Wellington Fund

Small and Medium US Stocks:
Vanguard Mid-Cap Index
Vanguard Small-Cap Index
Vanguard Explorer Fund

International/Non-US Stocks:
Vanguard Core International Stock Fund

Vanguard Emerging Markets Select Stock Fund

Bonds:
Total Bond Market Index
Vanguard High Yield Corporate Fund
Total International Bond Index

Real Estate:
Vanguard Real Estate Index
Vanguard Global ex-U.S. Real Estate Index

Now that we've got our library formed, let's look how to use it to design portfolios for different purposes. The considerations when building a portfolio are:

1. How much time you have until you need the money
2. How much risk and volatility you are willing to accept/handle
3. How much complexity and control you desire to have

On the third point, realize that this isn't an exact science and there are a lot of choices that will give you about the same results. The important thing is to be investing and putting money away. The level of fine-tuning you want to do is then up to you.

Chapter 2: Sample Portfolios

We will now go through several example portfolios, including how these portfolios are adjusted as time passes and you get closer to needing the money. We start with retirement investing since that is the main reason most people invest.

A Portfolio for Retirement Investing

Investment Horizon: 25-45 years

With the advent of 401Ks, investing for retirement has become the most popular reason for investing. Retirement requires so large an amount of money that it can be overwhelming, but it is very possible to amass plenty of money for a comfortable retirement if you use investing and start early. Assuming that you're starting to invest in your 20s or 30s, you have the time required to get the higher returns offered by the more volatile investments. Inflation is your biggest enemy with such a long time horizon, so you need to be fully invested all of the time and avoid keeping any money in bank assets like CDs. A possible portfolio from the library is as follows:

- Growth Index:12%
- Windsor Fund:13%
- Small-Cap Index:30%
- International Core Stock Fund:30%
- REIT Index:15%

Features of this portfolio are:

1. You're diversified among US stocks, large and small, growth and income, international stocks, and REITs. Each of these investments are volatile, meaning it will be difficult to predict their performance for the next five to ten years, but they should outperform other investments over longer periods of time unless something radical happens to the financial markets.
2. You slightly overweight the areas that have done better historically: value stocks and small stocks. You have separate growth and value funds instead of a blended fund so you can control the mix.
3. You have no bonds because their return will lag that of stocks over such a long period of time.

This is the portfolio you would buy and maintain while you still have at least 15 years until retirement when you'll be using the money. Once you got within 15 years, you'd start to add bonds, maybe ending up with something like this 15 years out:

- Growth Index:15%
- Windsor Fund:15%
- Small-Cap Index:20%
- International Core Stock Fund:25%
- REIT Index:15%
- Long-Term Corporate Bond Index:5%
- Wellesley Income Fund:5%

You've now added 10% bond and income funds, the Long-

Term Corporate Bond Index and the Wellesley Income Fund, since you're getting closer to when you need the money and therefore want to reduce portfolio volatility. You don't know whether stocks or bonds will outperform over a 15 year period, although it is extremely likely that stocks will outperform. You therefore maintain the ratio of stocks to bonds decidedly tilted towards stocks, but add a few bonds and income stocks just in case.

Note also that you've reduced your exposure to small stocks relative to large stocks and balanced out growth and income. Again, over shorter periods of time, whether large or small stocks and whether growth or income will win out is anyone's guess. You maintain a 15% exposure to REITs since they balance out both stocks and bonds and provide income in addition to capital appreciation.

You would continue to add bonds as you get closer to retirement age and reduce your risk. Standard advice ascribed to Jack Bogle, founder of Vanguard, is to invest your age in bonds. A person who was 65 would therefore have 65% bonds and 35% stocks. This advice has been revised, however, to invest your age minus 10% in bonds since people are living longer and you need to keep that exposure to equities (stocks) to keep up with inflation for a 30 or 40-year retirement. A portfolio when you're 60 and planning to retire at 65 might therefore look like this:

- Growth Index:10%
- Windsor Fund:10%

- Small-Cap Index: 5%
- International Core Stock Fund: 15%
- REIT Index: 10%
- Long-Term Corporate Bond Index: 30%
- Wellesley Income Fund: 20%

Here you've moved 50% of your investments into bonds and income assets (the income from which you should mainly be reinvesting). You've lightened up on small stocks since they are more volatile than large stocks. Finally, you still have an exposure to both REITs and international stocks to reduce volatility. This portfolio should be throwing off quite a bit of income in the way of dividends and interest. You can use some of that income to build up cash for upcoming expenses, but when you start spending the interest from a bond position, you'll be locking in the amount of cash you'll receive from that point forward. If you're getting $10,000 per year today, you'll be getting $10,000 per year in 25 years when you can only buy half as much with it. You should therefore be reinvesting cash you don't need in the near future.

Retirement Investing 102

The portfolios above represent the basic retirement investing strategy, the "Retirement Investing 101," if you will. But there are some tweaks that can be made along the way based on your situation and significant events that may occur. One such event is a period of extraordinarily high interest rates, as happened in the United States in the early 1980s. Paul Volker was running the Federal Reserve and trying to quash the hyperinflation that was occurring, so he raised rates to extraordinary levels, pushing bond yields and even bank CD rates sky-high. The Fed-Funds rate in 1980 was 13.35% and the Prime Rate was 15.26%. You could get 10-year treasury bonds paying 14% and even bank CDs paying over 12%. Aaa corporate bonds - those from companies with the highest quality and the lowest risk - were paying more than 15%! It was truly an exceptional time for income investors (and terrible for home buyers).

In that type of environment where bond interest payments and even bank CDs are paying more than the long-term average return for stocks, it makes sense to shift some of your money into bonds early. Maybe even put some of your money into the longest term bank CDs you can buy since it is an almost guaranteed return. Note that because the price of bonds would have fallen as rates rose, you would also be able to get substantial capital gains on your bond investments as they mature. You might have been able to buy bonds for $250 each that would mature in ten years and pay you $1000 each, all the while paying out $40 each a year in interest payments. It's tough to beat that with stocks.

Another special situation is where you have way more money than you need for retirement when you get there. In this case, you may decide to treat the portion of the portfolio you really need like you would if that were all the money you had (following the guidance from Retirement 101), and then leave the rest invested in stocks and REITs like you would when you were in your 20s. The thinking here is that you can afford to take the risk of a big 40% plunge in that portion of the portfolio since you don't really need the money.

If a big drop does occur, you can just leave it alone and wait a few years for it to recover, using the remainder of your portfolio for living expenses. You'd be no worse off if a big plunge happened than someone who had just enough for retirement. Conversely, when you have a big year in stocks, you can sell off some stocks and either use it for something special like a trip or a home addition, or add to your income portfolio and increase your income. This is a great situation to be in, and you can easily be here if you start investing early and putting away a good portion of your income for retirement (like 10%-15% per year).

Note an issue with this strategy is that if stocks have a really bad time like they did in the early 2000s with the bursting of the internet bubble in 1999 and then the housing collapse in 2008, you could actually have done better with the standard stock-bond portfolio than you did by concentrating in stocks. The annualized return for the S&P 500 was actually a negative 0.95% from January 2000 - Dec 2009.[1] As a result, you would have actually done better putting your money in a bank CD for the period. These types of periods are rare, however, and you actually would have had opportunities in 2006-2008 to sell portions of your portfolio and make a gain. If you were able to hold past 2009, you would have also seen phenomenal returns

---

1
. Dimensional Fund Advisors, *The Best and Worst of Times*, https://www.evidenceinvestor.com/the-best-and-worst-of-times/

in the 2010s. Part of using this kind of strategy is taking advantage of opportunities as they present themselves. If you have a good year where stocks are up, sell a portion. If you have a bad year where they decline substantially, just hold on. Because you don't need the money, you have flexibility. we'll talk more about this when we discuss income portfolios.

A final tweak involves reducing your risk when you're near retirement by converting to cash assets (bank CDs and short-term bond funds). This isn't something you want to do long-term because inflation will eat you alive, but if you need the money in a few years, taking advantage of a good year in the stock market to lock in some gains and convert to some cash is a wise move. Otherwise, if interest rates spike and you have stocks, bonds, and REITs, you can see your portfolio value decline quickly, forcing you to sell off depreciated assets early in retirement. This is one of the times where you risk running out of money late in retirement even if you have what should be enough to make it through. Having enough cash to make it a few years without needing to sell assets nearly eliminates this risk. If you have money in bank CDs and interest rates rise suddenly, you won't see a loss of principle and you can even roll the money from the CDs you have that have a lower interest rate locked in into new CDs at a higher rate and increase your income. Once again, we'll discuss this strategy further when we talk about income investing.

A Portfolio for College Investing

Besides retirement, college is probably the biggest expense

many families face. At the time of this writing in-state public college can easily cost $80,000 for a bachelor's degree. A private university can cost $300,000 or more due to its high, unsubsidized tuition. Many families therefore save and invest for this expense. The time horizon is long enough - if you start early - to take advantage of investing to reduce how much you need to put away yourself.

As an aside, I'll be honest here: Saving for college may not be right for everyone. The issue is that the need-based scholarships and financial aid turn college into a variable expense that equals "whatever you can pay." Private universities regularly give out tuition breaks such that very, very few people actually pay the full cost of tuition. Harvard may have a price tag of $60,000 per year, but maybe 5% of the students actually pay that. Others pay $20,000 per year, or $5000 per year, or nothing. If you put money away into a college savings account, however, that counts strongly against you when your kids apply for financial aid. If there are two families earning $60,000 per year and one sacrifices to put away $5000 per year, such that they have $150,000 for college in an account when their child turns 18, while the other puts away nothing and instead spends $5000 on car payments to buy new cars every three years, the college will likely say "thank you very much" to the first family and take the $150,000 while charging substantially less to the second family.

A much fairer system would be to charge tuition based on family income during the ten or 15 years before the child goes to school and during the time they are in classes. A child would then receive a break on tuition when they come from a family that could not afford to save for college, not just one that chose not to save. This would not penalize families who save and actually give an incentive for all families to put money away for college, reducing the cost for everyone.

Still, it is what it is, and because of that it would be wise when your child is young to spend some time with a financial planner and/or do some research into financial aid rules before you start saving and investing. Despite the tax savings, you may find that you're better off not using a college savings account or putting investments in the child's name under a custodial account since that counts against financial aid more strongly than if you invest in your own account and then pay for college from it. That said, if you do choose to invest for college for your children, the methodology to invest for such an expense is provided.

College saving is like retirement investing ten to eighteen years out from retirement. As such, when the child is born, you'll want to create a portfolio like:

- Growth Index: 20%
- Windsor Fund: 20%
- Small-Cap Index: 20%
- International Core Stock Fund: 20%
- REIT Index: 20%

Because you have 18 years until you'll start drawing on the

money, you can go ahead and allocate 100% to stocks and REITs. You would tilt towards larger stocks for their added stability since you don't have as long to invest as you would for retirement, but you still include a small-cap portion. As you get to 12 to 15 years out, you might shift to something like:

- Growth Index:25%
- Windsor Fund:25%
- Small-Cap Index:10%
- International Core Stock Fund:20%
- REIT Index:20%

Here you're cutting out volatility by reducing small caps, but still not adding bonds because you still have quite a ways to go. Note also that you should be investing additional money each year, which will mean that you'll be buying more when prices dip, lowering your cost basis and increasing your gains. As you get within 10 years of college, you'll add bonds:

- Growth Index:20%
- Windsor Fund:20%
- Small-Cap Index:10%
- International Core Stock Fund:20%
- REIT Index:10%
- Long-Term Corporate Bond Index:10%
- Wellesley Income Fund:10%

Of course, you'll be reinvesting the income you receive from the bonds and income fund since you don't need the money yet. As you go from ten to five years you'll be slowly increasing income investments and reducing equities, perhaps holding this portfolio five years out:

- Growth Index:15%
- Windsor Fund:15%
- Small-Cap Index:5%
- International Core Stock Fund:15%
- REIT Index:10%
- Long-Term Corporate Bond Index:20%
- Wellesley Income Fund:20%

At that point, you might stop reinvesting cash from the income investments and any dividends and capital gains distributions you receive, instead letting a cash position build up so that you'll be ready for the first tuition bills. A few years from college you might therefore have a portfolio like this:

- Bank CDs/short-term bond funds: 10%
- Growth Index:13%
- Windsor Fund:13%
- Small-Cap Index:4%
- International Core Stock Fund:10%
- REIT Index:10%
- Long-Term Corporate Bond Index:20%
- Wellesley Income Fund:20%

Notice that you don't get rid of stocks entirely. This is because having some stocks actually reduces your risk when compared to an all-bond portfolio and because you won't need all of the money on day one of college. If there were a market decline three years out from college starting, you could use the cash that you have to cover tuition the first year and then wait a bit to sell assets to raise cash for year two rather than selling depreciated assets.

As the final years tick by, you would add to the cash position and sell off the stock positions. When your child was ready to enter college, the portfolio might look like this:

- Bank CDs/short-term bond funds: 25%
- Growth Index: 5%
- Windsor Fund: 5%
- Small-Cap Index: 2%
- International Core Stock Fund: 5%
- REIT Index: 8%
- Long-Term Corporate Bond Index: 25%
- Wellesley Income Fund: 25%

You have a good cash reserve to pay for tuition and room and board for the first couple of years. With time you would then sell off stocks to replace cash you were spending and then finally bonds and REITs as you get near the end of the account and, hopefully, near the end of college.

A Portfolio for Current Income Investing

The main reason people are interested in investing for current income is that they are in retirement and need to generate money for expenses. Their portfolio becomes their income source, replacing their employer, and they need to have the money in their bank accounts replenished so they can cover their bills. There are other reasons where you might want to generate current income, however, such as paying for college, enhancing your lifestyle by adding investing income to your paycheck, paying for a recurring expense such as regular medical care for a condition, or maybe paying for special luxuries such as a yearly vacation. The goal of an income portfolio is to generate the income needed without depleting the assets in the portfolio, at least for the period of time over which it is being used.

Income investing is easier when interest rates are high enough that you can generate the money you need from interest and dividends without taking on excessive risk. You don't want rates to be too high, however, as that causes economic contractions and makes companies more likely to default on bonds. You're hoping to be in that sweet spot where rates are high enough for you to generate the needed income but low enough for the economy to keep chugging along and your interest payments to be paid.

Of course, the amount of income your portfolio can generate depends on how large your portfolio is. If you have a million dollar portfolio and safe, Aaa bond funds are paying 5% interest, you can generate $50,000 per year if you invested it all in such bond funds. If you did so, however, and spent all $50,000 each year, your spending power would decline over time. Instead, you might invest some of the money in stocks to keep up with inflation and only have $30,000 per year to spend. If that is enough money for your expenses, you'd be set. If interest rates were low such that you could only generate $10,000 per year with a Aaa bond fund, however, you would need to come up with more creative ways to generate the income you needed.

So, the first requirement in designing an income portfolio is to determine how much income you need and how much you can generate from income investments with the money you have. Let's say that you have $2M to invest at the start of retirement and the funds in your library are paying as follows:

- Bank CDs/short-term bond funds: 3%
- Growth Index: 0.1%
- Windsor Fund: 0.2%
- Small-Cap Index: 0.3%
- International Core Stock Fund: 1%
- REIT Index: 8%
- Long-Term Corporate Bond Index: 10%
- Wellesley Income Fund: 7%

You want to make sure your portfolio value grows over time so that your income will increase to keep up with inflation. Otherwise you'll be effectively losing spending power every year and be in trouble in 30 years when you can only buy half as much as you can now. You therefore keep a portion in stocks. You also want to have some cash-on-hand in case interest rates spike and your stock and bond portfolios decline right at a time when you have some big expense due. Having some cash also allows you to invest more in stocks and bonds

while they are cheap after an interest rate spike.
An investment allocation is such a scenario, right at the start of a standard retirement, for example, might be something like this:

- Bank CDs/short-term bond funds: 4%
- Growth Index: 10%
- Windsor Fund: 10%
- Small-Cap Index: 5%
- International Core Stock Fund: 15%
- REIT Index: 16%
- Long-Term Corporate Bond Index: 20%
- Wellesley Income Fund: 20%

Given the interest rates presented earlier, this portfolio would be generating $99,900 per year in income. If this were more than you needed, you could be reinvesting the additional income back into the various funds. For example, if you only needed $80,000 per year, you could be adding the additional $19,900 each year to the income-generating funds if you wanted to keep increasing your current income, or be directing money back into the stock funds if you wanted to increase growth for the future. This portfolio includes 40% bonds, 16% REITs, and 40% stocks, so it would hold up well under market volatility and also continue to grow in value over time, keeping up with inflation. You also have about $80,000 in cash assets, more than a year's worth of expenses, so you have pretty good coverage for whatever expenses may appear even if an event that caused the whole portfolio to drop like an interest rate hike happened.

If interest rates stayed relatively high throughout your retirement, such that you continued to receive sufficient income from your investments to pay for expenses, you would just periodically sell off some of the stocks and add to the bonds and income funds as time passed to preserve your spending power. If you retired at age 65 and lived to be 100, the portfolio might look like this:

- Bank CDs/short-term bond funds: 4%
- Growth Index: 5%
- Windsor Fund: 5%
- Small-Cap Index: 1%
- International Core Stock Fund: 5%
- REIT Index: 10%
- Long-Term Corporate Bond Index: 40%
- Wellesley Income Fund: 30%

If the portfolio had grown in size to $3M during the 35 years and income distribution rates for the funds remained the same, you would be receiving about $213,000 in income each year at that point. After inflation this would be equivalent to the portfolio being worth about $1.5M and paying out about $105,000 in income each year, just a little above the spending power that you started with when you started retirement on a slightly smaller portfolio. Of course, because you are seeing the value of the portfolio decline slowly over time, you would either need to cut how much you're spending or eventually it would run out. You might need to go back into the workforce at age 125.

The Income Investing Mindset

When you are investing for current income, it helps to change your mindset when looking at the value of your portfolio. When you were investing in growth stocks and trying to grow your portfolio, portfolio value was the thing that you tracked. When you are investing for current income, portfolio value matters less. Instead, you should be focused on how much income you are generating.

For example, an income fund that I have owned for more than 30 years is the DNP Select Income Fund, which has the symbol "DNP." If I were to look at a chart of this fund from a growth investor perspective, I would think it to be a lousy investment. Going all the way back to 1990, the fund's price has been flat. It started the period at about $11 per share and at the time of this writing it is at about $10.50 per share. It has been as high as $13 per share and as low as about $6 per share, both extrema happening within about the last 12 years. In general the range for the fund's price was from about $8 per share to $11.50 per share. From bottom to top this is about a 40% price swing, but it is nothing compared to the price changes you'd see in a stock growth fund over such a long period.

If I were focused in on the price, however, and bought in at $11 per share, I might get worried if I saw the share price drop down to $8 per share. If I had invested $100,000 in the fund, my investment would now have a value of $73,000, a loss of $27,000. Given that the fund pays out about $0.78 per share per year, or $7090 per year for my position of just over 9000 shares, it would take about four years of payments to make up for the loss in share price!

The key, however, is not to focus in on the share price but instead to focus on the income I am receiving. In my example I was receiving about $7090 when I bought in at $11 per share, and I am still receiving about $7090 per share now that the shares are priced at $8 per share. My investment is worth less, but the effective interest rate I am receiving is more, so I am still generating the same amount of income. If you go way back, you'll find that this fund has consistently generated about the same amount per share. In fact, if you look back all the way to 2013 you'll see that the fund has had a cash payout of $0.065 per share per month every month up through today.[2] There is also typically a distribution of any capital gains the fund has generated at the end of the year in December. The fund does this by creating a payout that they feel they can sustain each month, returning part of my investment to me in months where they don't generate enough income from their investment, but then keeping some in reserve when they generate more. They do this since investors who want current income like to have a steady stream rather than have large variances. Note that because the dollar amount they pay has been fixed, I would need to be reinvesting some of the return I am receiving or my spending power would decline over time.

---

2 . https://www.nasdaq.com/market-activity/stocks/dnp/dividend-history

So, if I focus on the income I am receiving rather than the value of the investment, my picture changes. I don't care that my investment is only worth $73,000 now instead of the $100,000 I invested because I am not planning to sell the fund anytime soon. The fund is continuing to generate the income that I need, so the price of the fund really has no bearing on me. I know that sometime in the future, if I wait long enough, the fund price will probably go back up to $11 per share. If I wanted to sell off some shares to buy something else or simply spend it on something, I could get back my full investment at that time. In the meantime, however, I keep collecting the income checks each month. When the fund gets back to $11 per share I'm not back to even, I'm way ahead of where I was when I bought it because I received all of those dividends. In fact, if I don't need the money right now I could be buying more shares while the stock is at $8 by reinvesting the dividends than I could have at $11 per share and then have my position worth substantially more when the fund does go back to $11.

It is unlikely that I'll ever sell the shares of DNP I have since they just keep doing what I want them to do - provide a steady stream of income. If I ever did want to sell, however, I could wait for a period when interest rates were low and sell at that time to take the capital gain. While I'm waiting, I'm collecting about 8% interest per year.

Other Current Income-Generation Options

We've already discussed some of the common income

generating options like the Vanguard Total Bond and REIT mutual funds, but there are several other fund types that can be considered. There are many funds designed for income investors like DNP that pay regular monthly payments instead of paying four times per year. That can be helpful if you have regular monthly bills. Some also have an equity portion so that they will increase in value somewhat if stocks are going up to help keep up with inflation. Most of these funds will issue a capital gain distribution at the end of the year, so you'll get a little extra income in December each year.

Like DNP, many of these funds invest in companies with high dividends or bonds of varying lengths. One such example is the Duff & Phelps Utility and Corporate Bond Trust (DUC), which pays a dividend of $0.05 per month of about $0.60 per year. Another possibility, especially when interest rates are low and bond and dividend funds aren't paying very well, is to invest in a buy-write fund. Here the fund manager will buy a set of stocks and then write *option contracts* against them. These are legal contracts that grant the buyer the ability to purchase the shares of stock for a prespecified price before a specified date in exchange for paying the writer (your fund) a premium. This limits the amount of capital appreciation the writer can get, but creates what is effectively a dividend payment on the stocks in the account. An example of such a fund is the Eaton Vance Tax-Managed Buy-Write Opportunities Fund (ETV). This fund has distributed $1.33 per year for the last several years, which is equivalent to about an 8.8% yield at this point in time. This fund also makes payments once per month.

A Portfolio for Generating Income from Capital Gains

The income investing scenario presented above was a fairly ideal time period where interest rates are high enough that you can generate enough income to pay for things from interest payments and dividends while investing enough to sustain the value of the portfolio with inflation. (Note also that you saved up $2M over your working lifetime for retirement, which also made things fairly easy. If you only had $500,000 saved up, you would either need to take a lot of risk in your investments to generate more income or cut your yearly income from the portfolio dramatically. It is really important to be saving and investing all throughout your career, and avoid raiding your retirement accounts or taking loans from your 401k while you are working. Start early and invest consistently. Your future self will thank you.) But what if interest rates were really low when you were ready to retire, or what if they dip way down while you are retired? How can you generate the income you need?

The answer is that you can generate the income you need from capital gains instead of from interest and dividend paying assets. This is more risky than using income-generating assets, but may be your only option if you retire in a very low interest rate environment. You can cut your risk by building up a fairly substantial amount of cash in the account, such that you don't need to take money out of the markets when stocks take a big dip. You can also use funds that use option writing like ETV since the income generating capabilities of these funds will not be affected by low interest rates.

An example portfolio for this strategy might look as follows:

- Bank CDs/short-term bond funds: 10%
- Growth Index: 20%
- Windsor Fund: 15%
- Small-Cap Index: 5%
- International Core Stock Fund: 20%
- REIT Index: 10%
- Buy-Write Funds 10%
- Wellesley Income Fund: 10%

You have a relatively large cash position (Bank CDs and short-term bond funds). If you had $2M in the portfolio, this would be $200,000 in cash assets, enough to cover about five years' worth of expenses at $40,000 per year. You would also be getting some income from the REIT Index Fund, buy-write funds, and Wellesley Income Fund so you wouldn't just have your cash position to spend.

With this portfolio, you would need to take advantage of market movements to raise more cash. If you have a good year and the market moves up, you would sell off some shares of the stock funds and replace some of the money you were spending. If you have a bad year where the market falls, you would just use the cash you have and wait for things to improve. This avoids the biggest risk to a retirement portfolio: Running out of money due to a big drop in the markets at the start of retirement, forcing you to sell your stocks and bonds at low prices. Because most market drops recover within a couple of years, if you have enough cash on hand to meet expenses for several years, you are protected from the sharp but short-lived declines that occur every ten to twenty years.

Like anything else, you'll want to have a firm plan in place when using this strategy. For example, start out with enough cash to last you for five years without touching the stock and bond accounts. Then, each year in January (after stocks have made their typical run-up in the fall), if your portfolio has increased in value by at least 10%, sell enough shares to add a couple of years to your cash position. If it is up between 0 and 10%, sell enough to regain the year and add to your cash position so you're back where you started the year. If it is down, sit pat for the next year and use your cash and income from your income funds for expenses.

Have a limit below you'll not allow your cash position to drop, maybe 2 or 3 years. If this does happen, go ahead and sell some shares even if the market is down and you're doing so at a depressed prices. Note that the amount of cash you'll need will increase over time with inflation, so you may start out at $200,000 at age 65 but be at $400,000 when you're 85.

This is the strategy if you start out retirement when interest rates are low. If interest rates start low but then increase while you are retired, this will likely cause your stock and income funds to decline in price, at least initially. The percentage your income funds are paying, however, will increase as their price drops, plus bond funds will drop in price and start paying higher interest rates. If this happens, you can start using some of the cash you have to buy bond funds since now you may start receiving enough income from these funds to pay for things. You can invest down to maybe 1-2 years' worth of cash. Even the short-term bond funds and CDs will start paying out more interest, so your income on the cash assets you have will increase as well. Remember, your concern is having enough income, not what your funds are worth at any given time. Stock funds will likely start going back up in price after the initial shock of seeing interest rates rise, in which case you can also start to sell off some of these funds and put more into bonds, raising your income further.

A portfolio for future purchases

As a final example, let's say that you have a big future purchase coming up and you want to use investing as a way to reduce the amount you actually need to put away for the purchase. For example, let's say that you're replacing used cars every five years and you want to invest the money as you save for the next one. Here, because you would be saving as you go, you would want to build the portfolio as you put money away. To see how this works, let's say that you need $15,000 for the next car. You'd first save up the minimum to buy into a fund ($3000, for Vanguard Funds), then buy your first fund:

- $3000 Vanguard S&P 500 Fund

You started out with a large-cap stock fund since you are at the longest point before the purchase is made, so it makes sense to start with stocks. You want to balance things out with bonds, however, because you really don't know which will do best over such a short period. You then put the next $3000 in bonds. Let's say you've made 10% on the stock fund in the meantime. Your portfolio then looks like this:

- $3300 Vanguard S&P 500 Fund
- $3000 Vanguard Total Bond Index Fund

You would reinvest interest payments from the bond fund since you don't need the cash right away and want to maximize your growth. Next, you might mix in some REITs to keep your diversification high. After the third investment, it might look like this:

- $3500 Vanguard S&P 500 Fund
- $3050 Vanguard Total Bond Index Fund
- $3000 Vanguard Real Estate Index Fund

You now have about $10,000 invested for your $15,000 purchase. Let's say that you were putting $3000 per year away and it is now the end of year three with two more years to go. You would keep this ratio with everything balanced out at about ⅓ since you don't know what is going to perform the best during the period, so you would direct new investments to those funds that were lagging the others. You would want to be investing regularly from this point on since that would allow you to get a better price on the shares through dollar-cost averaging. So, if you were putting away $250 per month, you might send $150 to the fund lagging the other two, then $100 each to the other two funds. Note that you don't sell any funds since this is a taxable account and you don't want to trigger any capital gains taxes until you have no choice.

Now, let's say you're a year out and there is a big rally in the stock market, such that your portfolio now looks like this:

- $7400 Vanguard S&P 500 Fund
- $3350 Vanguard Total Bond Index Fund
- $4500 Vanguard Real Estate Index Fund

you now have $15,250 in the account. This includes $12,000 that you saved and invested and $3,250 from investment returns. You would now have enough for your car plus a bit left over to pay the taxes on your gains. You could then sell the funds and collect the cash. Since you're still a year out from the purchase, you would want to at least buy a 1-year CD to get as much interest as you could. You might even want to put a portion, maybe half, in a short-term bond fund since you could collect 3-4% instead of 0.5% in a CD, although that would just mean you'd get about $120 more for the slight additional risk you were taking. Given the risk, you might decide instead to just stick with the sure thing CD.

If you wanted to buy the next car in 5 years but didn't really need to buy the car at that point, you could go ahead and take the additional chance of leaving the money invested for that additional year. This could mean that you'd need to wait another year or two if there was a big drop in the markets during that year (especially if interest rates rise), but it could mean that you'd end up with another $1000 or even $2000. You are able to take this risk because you have flexibility of when you need to make the purchase, allowing you to take the money out when market conditions are best. You can use flexibility to mitigate the effects of market uncertainty.

Note, an even better situation is where you take the money for all of the big purchases that are coming up, like cars, new roofs, new air conditioning units, etc... and put away money for all of them as you go. You would then just keep 1/3rd of the money invested in each fund since you would not need the money for all three expenses at the same time. Instead, you would just keep contributing to this investment portfolio, adding to whichever fund was lagging the others at a given time, and then take out money as needed when expenses come up. If you knew that an expense was coming within a year and the markets did really well (like a year where the stock market goes up 30%), you would take out the money for that expense out early and put it in a CD, taking advantage of the opportunity you were given to lock in the gain.

Chapter 3: Managing Your Portfolios

Getting Started

If you're new to investing, certainly it can be kind of scary to send in your money and see the values or your portfolio go up and down. Realize, however, you have a lot on your side. Specifically:

1. The markets as a whole tend to go up over time
2. Most large drops are erased within a year or two
3. If you're sending in money regularly, you're buying at better prices when markets drop
4. If you keep investing, your gains will be far more than your losses

The best way to get started and learn how to invest is therefore to just start investing. You don't put a huge amount of money in to start, but getting some money into the markets and then adding to it is the best way to start to learn. Since you're using mutual funds and you stick with a buy and hold strategy, there is almost no risk of losing everything. (If you do, society has probably collapsed and we'll be fighting each other for food on the streets.) The main risk is that your rate of return will be less than it could have been. Accept that you might see your portfolio value go down after you make your first investment, but know that if you keep sending in money and investing it in a diversified set of stocks and other assets, you will see gains eventually. None of the fluctuations will matter until you're ready to pull the money out.

Trading is not your friend

In the 1990s and before you'd get an idea of how you were doing about once a day when you went through the closing prices of your stocks the next morning in the newspaper, or in the afternoon paper if you lived in the West where markets closed around 1 or 2 PM. You might also see your stock tick by with its closing price if you knew the symbol on a show like The Nightly Business Report on PBS.

Today we have constant updates on our stocks available through our phones and computers. This makes the process a lot more exciting and you do get a lot better idea of what is happening during the day, but that kind of information overload drives us to want to trade. You see yourself making $100, or $1000 or even $10,000 for the day and want to sell off. You see a stock you're interested in moving up and want to buy before it goes too high. You see a huge downturn, see all that you've made over the last several years being wiped out, and want to sell before you lose more. This is the kind of behavior that will destroy your returns.

You will get the highest returns by buying in at regular intervals and leaving everything alone. Then, when you're a couple of years away from needing the money, start selling off portions as the market presents opportunities until you have enough in cash for what you need. If you're investing for retirement, this means selling enough to have a cash position that can cover you for a few years and then selling to add to it as time passes to replenish what you're spending.

Managing your psychology

Your emotions are your worst enemy when it comes to investing. You'll want to buy at the worst possible times and, even worse, sell and sit on the sidelines right when the best opportunities present themselves. Paul Winkler, a financial advisor in the Nashville, TN area, periodically reviews the effect of sitting on the sidelines on investor returns. He has found that if you miss just a few of the most critical days – those where the markets go up dramatically – because you've pulled your money out because of fear of a downturn, you will get returns in the 2% range instead of the 10 to 12% buy and hold investors will see during the same period. When markets go up, they go up quickly over very short periods of time. The rest of the time they tread water and go nowhere. Over 40 years, at 12% you'd have $118,000 for every $1000 invested. At 2%, you'd have $2200.

The issue is that you'll be dealing with fear and greed. Some people lean more towards the fear side, others towards the greed, but we all have these impulses and they will affect our investment returns if we let them. Fearful people will not invest enough, lean too heavily on "safe" investments, sell out and take a loss when markets decline, and always be worrying about losing money. Greedy people will invest too aggressively for the time period they have, stay invested when they should be taking out cash, think that they can see things others don't and trade stocks to increase their returns, and always be looking at what they could have made if they had invested in a different mutual fund. Most people lean towards fear or greed, but can and do flip over in different stages of the market. During long bull markets, many get greedy. During brutal bear markets, many get fearful. This is exactly the opposite of the behavior that produces the best returns.

Control your greed and fear impulses by setting your mind in the right state for successful investing. This includes doing the following:

1. Accept that you cannot predict where the markets will go over the short term. The price of the markets already includes all knowledge that is out there.
2. Know that markets *will* decline in price on a regular basis and do so very quickly. If you hold stocks for 10 years, you should expect some of your mutual funds to decline by 20% to 40% two or three times during the period. Despite this, you can expect your portfolio value to double about every five to eight years, so the gains you see will be erased and you'll end up way better than you started if you hold on.
3. Because equity returns are predictable over short periods of time, money you really, really need within a few years should be in cash/bank CDs. Don't let your greed make you leave money invested that you really, really need.
4. If you're investing for long periods of time, look at market downturns as sales on stocks and other equities. These are the times to get greedy because the biggest returns occur when a downturn ends.

What you do and don't need to be doing

There are things you should be doing in managing your portfolio and things you shouldn't. Things you should do include:

1. Be adding money to increase your positions regularly. By buying at different times, you improve your cost basis (the amount you pay for shares), especially if you add the same dollar amount each time since then you'll be buying more shares when they're relatively cheap. This is called "dollar cost averaging." This also helps you stay calm in downturns since you'll know you're getting more shares cheap.
2. Periodically rebalance your portfolio, decreasing positions that have grown greater than your selected allocations and adding to positions that have decreased below them. Do this once or twice a year at most. As you get closer to the time when you need the money, adjust the allocations to each investment class appropriately as was shown in the sample portfolios.
3. Monitor your funds periodically to verify that they are still investing the way you expect. This is less looking at their performance than looking at what they are investing in and how well they are tracking the returns of the market they are meant to target. If small caps are up 20% but your small cap fund only returns 10%, you should investigate why.
4. Keep track of when you bought and what you paid. Many fund companies keep this info for you, but make

sure it is right and that you keep your own records if needed. You'll need this info for filing your taxes and for tax planning.
5. When possible if using a taxable account, add to funds with new cash when you need to increase your allocation instead of selling funds that have done well. When you sell funds that have appreciated, you may need to pay capital gains, so it is better to direct new investments to the areas you want to bulk up. Never, however, let taxes be a deciding factor on how you manage your portfolio since you will lose a lot more through market drops or missed gains than you will lose through taxes.

Things you shouldn't do are:
1. Sell and go to cash based on news you hear or what pundits are saying. Scary headlines bring in viewers and readers and pundits who are right when making a call (good or bad) get asked back to the talk shows. Everyone likes making calls of where the markets will go over the next few weeks or year but no one knows.
2. Shift your investments to the funds that did the best for a given period. It is easy to second guess yourself when you see that one fund has gone up 30% while another only went up 10% or is flat. Realize though that each segment of the markets will eventually make the historical returns for that segment. Shifting assets and buying funds that have done really well means you're putting more money in assets that have gone up, making them therefore less likely to post superior

returns in the future, while taking money out of the funds that are lower in price and therefore more likely to outperform In the future. Some areas will do nothing for five years and then go up 60% for the year all at once. Be patient.
3. Leave money invested that you really, really need. If you have some flexibility where you can wait a few years if a market swoon happens or if you have enough invested to sustain a big market drop and still have the cash you need, you can stay invested longer. If you really need the money at a certain date within a few years, however, go to cash with that portion of your portfolio.
4. Be checking your investments constantly. The more frequently you check, the more likely you are to make adjustments and make mistakes. Really, checking a few times per year is plenty. If things are going down and you're worried you'll do something rash, it's perfectly acceptable to just ignore things completely for a while.

Let automation help

There are some automated tools that can help you with portfolio management and with controlling your emotions. These are:

Auto-investment: Most mutual fund companies will let you set up automated deductions from your checking account to make regular investments. These help you actually stick to your investing plan and do dollar cost averaging to improve your cost basis.

Auto-rebalancing: Some companies allow you to set things up to automatically shift money among funds to maintain your desired allocations. This can be useful, but don't rebalance more than twice per year and don't do this if the money is in a taxable account. There you want more control to reduce your taxes.